Watch It Go

Go Train!

By Czeena Devera

The train is on the route.

The train is on the tracks.

The train is on the bridge.

The train is on the coast.

The train is on the water.

The train is in the forest.

The train is in the desert.

The train is in the country.

The train is in the city.

The train is in the mountain.

The train is in the tunnel.

The train is at the station.

Word List

train	water	mountain
route	forest	tunnel
tracks	desert	station
bridge	country	
coast	city	

72 Words

The train is on the route.
The train is on the tracks.
The train is on the bridge.
The train is on the coast.
The train is on the water.
The train is in the forest.
The train is in the desert.
The train is in the country.
The train is in the city.
The train is in the mountain.
The train is in the tunnel.
The train is at the station.

Published in the United States of America by Cherry Lake Publishing
Ann Arbor, Michigan
www.cherrylakepublishing.com

Photo Credits: © Mr. Klein/Shutterstock.com, front cover; ; © Leonid Andronov/Shutterstock.com, back cover, 1, 15; © Leonid Andronov/Shutterstock.com, 2; © BCFC/Shutterstock.com, 3; © Tobias Arhelger/Shutterstock.com, 4; © HTU/Shutterstock.com, 5; © Dominique de La Croix/Shutterstock.com, 6; © Giovanni Love/Shutterstock.com, 7; © Ahmad A Atwah/Shutterstock.com, 8; © remik44992/Shutterstock.com, 9; © Philip Lange/Shutterstock.com, 10; © Chilkoot/iStockphoto, 11; © Ivan Marjanovic/Shutterstock.com, 12; © Pagina/Shutterstock.com, 13

Cherry Blossom Press is an imprint of Cherry Lake Publishing.

Library of Congress Cataloging-in-Publication Data

Names: Devera, Czeena, author.
Title: Go train! / Czeena Devera.
Description: Ann Arbor, MI : Cherry Lake Publishing, 2019. | Series: Watch it go |
Includes bibliographical references and index. | Audience: Pre-school, excluding Kindergarten.
Identifiers: LCCN 2018034502| ISBN 9781534139190 (pbk.) | ISBN 9781534140394 (pdf) |
ISBN 9781534141599 (hosted ebook)
Subjects: LCSH: Railroad trains–Juvenile literature. | Reading (Preschool)
Classification: LCC TF148 .D48 2019 | DDC 625.2–dc23
LC record available at https://lccn.loc.gov/2018034502

Printed in the United States of America
Corporate Graphics

CHERRY BLOSSOM PRESS